Consc...

What I CHOOSE to BE
as I create me

An *Artists Lifeline* Publication

Conscious Choices

What I CHOOSE to BE as I create me

Celeste R. Pichette

An *Artists Lifeline* Publication

Published by Artists Lifeline, LLC,
    Honolulu, Hawai`i

Pichette, Celeste R.
    Conscious choices : what I choose to be as I create
    me / Celeste R. Pichette
    ISBN-13: 978-0983149217
    ISBN-10: 0983149216

Originally published as an ePub
    by Celeste R. Pichette

Printed in the United States of America

Dedication

This book is dedicated to my son Christopher.

From the day you were born, you have been my mirror always reflecting me back to myself. You have been my constant companion and bearer of wisdom when I needed it most. Your entry into this world woke me up from a long unconscious slumber, and your presence has guided my choices and journey to places it may never have gone without you in my life.

You have been, and always will be, the greatest gift I ever received from God.

Thank you for choosing me and honoring me with the role of being your mother.

Acknowledgements

My heartfelt gratitude to:

Sharon, Kim and Joanne, my initial editors, oh so many years ago.

George, for the use of your father's pictures, and for calling me "Pollyanna", providing added motivation.

Rose, for your continual encouragement and support year after year, and for always asking, "What are you doing with your book?"

Marilyn, my editor, for moving the book from its conversation style to proper English.

Bill, my designer and illustrator, for giving the book a face with your cover design, and for adding your artistic flare to the circle diagrams. Contact Bill at *bill.rehahn@gmail.com.*

Pat and Brad, my business partners, for embarking on this publishing journey with me. It would not have happened without you.

Oneliners & Proverbs *http://www.oneliners-and-proverbs.com* and Cyber Nation International, Inc. *http://www.cybernation.com*, for providing the supportive quotes.

Marianne, for facilitating the beginning of my transformation, *http://www.marianneweidlein.com*

My parents, for bringing me into the world. As I told you when I celebrated my 40th birthday, "I pray parenthood has been all you hoped it would be."

Craig, my "little" bro, for allowing me to love like a parent long before I was one.

Joanne, Pat, and Mary Ann, my soul sisters. I look forward to many more road-trips.

Patrick, for the ways your life touched mine so often and in so many ways while you embodied the physical realm. I still feel your presence at each choice point. I'm grateful for the choices we made this time and I see the perfection in the journey.

Contents

Prologue

Like most people on the planet, I'm a sucker for a good story. I love story-telling. So when I sat down to write this book, I could not resist telling my own story of how I arrived at this point in my life.

This book is about Choices. It is a guide for remembering how these wonderful things called choices really make our life what it is and give us our purpose for being here. Since it is a book designed to help a person create who they want to be, it is not essential that you know my story. So guess what? You have a choice. You can choose to:

1. read the rest of the Prologue called "Taking Over the Cockpit of Life and Remembering How to Fly," and then go on with the rest of the book, or

2. skip right to Chapter 1: Choices, start using the book for its intended purpose and not worry about who wrote it, or

3. complete option 2 and then come back and find out who wrote the book, or

4. skip right to Chapter 5: The Process, if you believe you have a thorough understanding of choices, and then move through the process of creating yourself, or

5. complete option 4 and then come back and find out who wrote the book.

Bet you never thought there were so many choices when reading a book, huh?

Taking Over the Cockpit of Life and Remembering How to Fly:

You may be wondering who I am or how I arrived at this point in my life. Let me tell you I did not get here by getting a degree in psychology, theology, philosophy, or any other "ology". I arrived here through my life – lived. It is only in the past few years that I have come to understand what I am writing about. Once I began to understand these ideas and see their implication in my life, I could not keep them to myself. I had to share them. There is an ever-growing desire inside of me to help as many people as possible to remember who they really are and live their greatest potential, if that is what they desire. As I evolve, my greatest potential, or vision for my life, evolves as well. The purpose of my life is to always be defining and re-defining (choosing and re-choosing) what my vision is and creating it in my life.

I certainly have not lived my life making the conscious choices I discuss throughout this book or exhibiting this kind of wisdom. No, my life is probably pretty similar to the lives of thousands of people on the planet. Honestly, I began to truly live my life only a decade ago. At the age of 30, I was one who "appeared" to have it all together: intelligent, college-educated, good job in my chosen profession, new beautiful home, nice suburban neighborhood, close-knit family, husband, beautiful and healthy 2-year-old baby boy. Yes, on the surface I had it all. But I remember one August evening, sitting down and having a very deep conversation with my best friend about our marriages and our futures. As we both opened up to each other, it appeared that we were in similar places in our marriages. By the end of our discussion, we were even finishing each other's sentences. There was no communication in our marriages. The kids had become the central focus of the marriages. We were spending too much time at work. Where were we going? What were we doing? On and on the comparisons went.

I remember saying to her,

> "Karen, when I look into the future, I don't see my husband and myself together. I see just Christopher and me, or sometimes I just see me alone. It's so scary, so empty."

At that point in my life, I was not a person who looked into or planned too far into the future. I did not live my life with a 5-year and 10-year plan. Visualization was a concept and a practice I had not yet discovered.

Little did I know that exactly one year later I would be moving out of my beautiful home, away from my husband, away from the neighborhood that seemed so much like the one I had grown up in, and most painfully moving away from my son at least on a part-time basis. I was facing what in my mind was the unthinkable in life – a divorce. While divorce may not be the greatest tragedy in a person's life (I can think of worse), it ranks high on the list of life stresses. To some, my divorce would appear to have been a cakewalk in comparison to what others have faced during their divorces. Nonetheless it was a painful experience that ran high on emotions and choices.

4

I had been the good little Catholic girl all my life: straight A's, honor-roll, athletic, extra-curricular activities, scholarship, respectful, polite, the picture of what every parent would want. I met my husband at my freshman orientation in college. He was two years older and a group leader. We dated all through college. Actually, we were attached at the hip. Being innocent and naïve, I thought that was how it was supposed to be when you were "in love".

We were engaged the spring of my senior year and set a wedding date for two years later. When we announced our engagement, the reaction from most of our college friends was, "It's about time." I had long since lost contact with my few friends from high school. Once we became a couple in 1988, it seemed that my high school friends and I were heading in different directions. I was too wrapped up in my new life of campus living and being a couple. During our dating years, we only had mutual friends. If you knew him, you knew me. If you knew me, you knew him. Our identity was defined as a couple. We had lost our individual identities. Since I met him as soon as I left home, which is when I thought I would finally find my identity, I did not lose my individual identity because I never had one. I subconsciously created my identity by defining myself as his other half. Similarly I had subconsciously created my former identity as the perfect daughter to my parents, student to my teachers, and good little girl to the rest of the world. I did not know who I was and I was too scared to try to find out. I let everyone else define who I was.

This realization led me to be adamant about WHO was making the choices in my life. You can tell from my own life synopsis, I was not making conscious choices. I let life happen and I let others lead me.

After my divorce, I finally took the journey to discover who I was. I participated in nearly two years of counseling and I read numerous spiritual books. The one constant in my life was my relationship with God. As I look back, even that seemed to be on the back burner during my marriage. Going to church every Sunday hardly made my faith the focal point of my life. I was too wrapped up in daily life, always busy and always doing, doing, doing.

Once the trouble in the marriage became unbearable, I moved my faith right to the front burner. I was always praying and, for the first time in my life, I began to listen too. It is amazing what you can hear when you open up to the possibility that God will actually communicate with you. My divorce was the most difficult challenge I ever faced in life but it provided me with an opportunity for spiritual and self-growth that I never thought possible. My strong faith in God is by far what sustained me through this <u>more than anything or anyone</u>. However, on my journey I discovered a deeper faith not only in God but in myself. Through all of this I have grown and matured in areas of myself that I did not know existed. It has been a soul-searching journey of self-discovery. I have conquered issues with other relationships, past experiences, and things about myself that I would never have had the courage to face without this experience. I learned to both love and trust myself for the first time in my life. I am finally discovering who I really am and who I want to be. The journey is by no means over. In fact, I have come to know that it is not a journey of self-discovery but rather a process of self-creation.

It is my hope that this book will help others to understand how they can self-create the life they choose. With faith in God and in yourself, a person can endure any situation or challenge. Everything may not turn out as you may have planned or hoped, but with faith in yourself, trust in who you are, and God by your side, you will get through whatever you are facing.

I made a very important choice with my divorce. I chose the impact it would have on my life. Would it be positive or negative? You will see that I chose positive. I chose to make my divorce a growth experience. I made myself the pilot flying this thing called life and, yes, God is my co-pilot and navigator. I would have it no other way.

Chapter 1:

Choices

What kind of choices have you made today? This week? This month? This year? This lifetime?

Why did you make the choices you made?

Would you call the choices good or bad? Did you get the results you expected? Did you have expectations when you made the choices?

Did your choices serve you? Did they help you evolve into who you really are?

This little book will help you work through these questions and illustrate a process that you can incorporate into your daily life if you choose to experience a higher expression of who you think you are. If you so choose, it will show you how to create, and thus experience, that higher self that you intuitively know is hiding inside of you. That higher self is inside of you under all the misconceptions instilled in your mind by the outside world.

Picture an iceberg. Better yet, let me show you one.

Source Unknown

The portion of the iceberg that is below the water's surface is the portion of your higher self that you can choose to show the world or you can choose to hide from the world. The choice is yours.

Choices, what are they? We make them all the time every day, every minute: from when to get up in the morning, to what to wear to work, to whether to go to work, to what kind of work you do, to what kind of person you are while you are at work. Every action you perform is a choice. You can choose to act the way you are acting or you can choose not to. You can choose to act a certain way for another's benefit or you can choose to act for your own benefit. Your choice may be based on the beliefs of society, the beliefs of your religion, the beliefs of your education, the beliefs of your parents or a combination of these. Believe it or not your choices may be based on your own inner beliefs, those beliefs you have yet to discover.

Your choices are statements to the world of who you are. Who you are is a combination of all your thoughts, all your values, and all your experiences. However, that is who you are NOW. Who you will BE is the manifestation of the conscious choices you are going to make each day you wake up and realize that this lifetime was given to you by God for you to create who you choose to BE.

What is going on in your life at this moment, how your life is and how it will be is all up to you. You have the power within yourself to create the life you desire. The life you desire is directly related to where you are coming from when you make every decision in your life. Whether it is a small decision or a large one, when you make that decision from the space of who you are versus what you are doing you will experience a completely different outcome. This is because you are creating rather than reacting to what is happening in your life.

Let me give you an example. Christopher, my then 4½ year old son, and I were in the store buying a gift for a birthday party after a long day of work and school.

I said, "How about a Tonka truck since the theme of the party is construction workers?"

Christopher replied, "No, Michael doesn't want that."

He headed for the game aisle and quickly selected the Power Ranger game.

I asked, "Do you think that's something Michael would like to receive as a gift?"

He said, "Yes," and handed it to me.

I was quite surprised and grateful that this whole selection process took only about three minutes because I was hungry after a long work day. I was ready to go home, relax, and have dinner.

I said, "Great, let's go pay for this."

Christopher stood completely still.

I bent down to his eye-level and asked, "What's up?"

Without a word, and with the look of a child who knows he is pushing the limits, he took another box of the same game off the shelf, handed it to me, and pointed to himself. He had a way of turning into a mime when he knew he was asking for something he probably was not going to get. In that moment, I took a deep breath because I could see what was coming.

I softly and gently said, "Do you want a game for yourself?"

He shook his head "Yes."

"But we're here to get Michael's gift," I said gently, more to keep myself calm than to calm him.

Christopher immediately began to cry and say he wanted one for himself because he knew how to play it – as if that would justify me buying it. We were about to go into meltdown mode. I had a decision to make. I could lose patience with him based on what I was doing which was rushing, because I felt tired and hungry, OR I could BE patient with him. I consciously opted for the latter, choosing to create the outcome of this situation instead of reacting to something that was quickly going to be out of my control. I knew that if I remained patient and calm, that positive influence would overcome what he was doing – preparing to throw a tantrum.

Staying eye-level with him, I took a pen and paper out of my purse (thank God I had those in there).

I told Christopher, "I have an idea. We can start making your birthday list. This way, when it's your birthday and people ask what you want, you'll have a list of things you want but weren't able to get when you saw them."

He cried, "But I want it now. My birthday is far, far away."

Calmly, I said, "I know, sweetheart, but we are not getting you the game now, so this is a way for you to maybe get it in the future. Now, what else did you see here today that you might want to get for your birthday?"

Patiently, distracting him, I said, "How about the Rescue Heroes you saw the other day?"

He whined, "But, Mom..."

I smiled at him with all the patience I could muster. He thought for a minute. I'm not sure what was running through his mind but I could tell he was beginning to calm down. The tears stopped and he seemed to be contemplating his next move. I waited, patiently.

Finally he said, "Yeah, the Rescue Heroes." "Anything else?" I asked.

"No."

"Alright then, let's go pay for this."

He again stood still, not wanting to follow me as I took a few steps down the aisle.

Gently, I said, "Come on, let's go home so we have time to play baseball after dinner."

He waited, not responding, deciding whether he wanted to pursue the tantrum or not. I stood patiently waiting, and smiling, to see what decision he would make. Still wanting to control the situation but knowing he had lost the battle, he stood for a few more minutes, contemplating. Getting no reaction from me – or should I say no over-reaction – he finally started toward me and followed me to the checkout. Tantrum diverted, we peacefully went on with our evening.

If I had chosen to rush and react to Christopher, this situation would have turned out differently. I would have only "added fuel to fire", as the saying goes. I could have lost patience, grabbed him by the arm, pulled him down the aisle and yelled, "You are not getting the game. Let's go!!" If you have children or have ever been in a store you know what I mean. You have seen it – frazzled mother pulling kicking and screaming child out of the store, her anger and frustration building as she reacts to the child's anger.

What happened instead was that I came from a place of being patient and peaceful. This gave me the ability to create a different outcome, one that would serve each of us differently than the child's tantrum/frazzled mom scenario.

The ability to create a different outcome came from my continual, conscious choice to remain calm and patient. And, trust me, it was a continual process. I must have decided 15 times in that short 10-minute time frame to remain patient and calm. But in the end, I created a more peaceful outcome and utilized less physical and mental energy than if I had let him dictate my reaction to the situation. It took constant monitoring on my part to not give in to his emotions and react negatively to the situation.

Now, this was a very small – some would say insignificant – incident, but the basic principle can be applied to all of life.

That basic principle relates to _choice_ and to apply it to your life, you need to have a thorough understanding of choices: what are they, when are they made, how are they made, where do they lead to, why are they made, and most importantly WHO makes them?

Let's start with the last item, WHO makes choices? The answer may seem obvious – everyone. But does the WHO that is making the decision really know WHO they are, or are they hiding behind someone else? Is it really a decision you would make, or is it a decision society, religion, education, parents, spouse, or friends would make for you? Are you making decisions about your appearance based on society's view of the perfect body? Are you hiding the experience of your pre-marital sex because religion says you should not do that? Are you looking to the past for answers on how to handle current situations because that's what you learned in school? Are you staying in a job you hate because the economy is down and your parents have instilled in you the belief that you should be happy you have a job? Have you begun to discard your hobbies in favor of what your spouse likes and not your own? Do you live beyond your financial means just to keep up with the Joneses?

Getting to the root of who is really making the decision is sometimes the most difficult step. It requires you to be completely honest with yourself and to stop hiding out from yourself. Why are you making the choices you are making? Sometimes the honest answer to that question will lead you to realize YOU are not the one making the decision at all. You are allowing everyone else to influence your choices.

The institutions mentioned above – society, religion, family, friends, etc. – have and will contribute to WHO you are and what choices you will make. But you must be VERY CLEAR that you are the only person who can make choices for you. Even by letting someone else choose for you, you are making a decision to let that person lead you. In the end, it may lead you where you wanted to go but then again it may not. Unconscious decisions that get you into a difficult situation can give you the perfect scapegoat. Our thought may be: I am a "victim" of the choice that you made. When we allow another person to make a choice for us and things do not turn out the way we want, we might see ourselves as a victim. We give the responsibility of the decision to someone else, leaving us free and clear from whatever the results might be, good or bad. Generally, it is only when the outcome is viewed as "bad" that we see ourselves as the victim.

"You made the decision; now look what happened," we say to the other person.

"Everything that's going wrong for me is your fault."

We forget that we made a choice, too, the choice to let the other person make our decision for us. This leads into WHAT are choices?

Choices are statements to the world of who you are. These can be direct statements: I love children; therefore, I choose to be a teacher and influence the future of the planet. They can be indirect statements: I believe children are our future; therefore, I choose to contribute financially to organizations that promote the well-being of children.

Our choices can be large or small, difficult or easy to make, the result of much thought or spontaneous. Personally, I like small, easy, spontaneous choices, but that is not what we encounter most of the time.

Let's discuss WHEN choices are made. They are made every minute of every day. Every minute of every day you are doing something. You may be sleeping, eating, reading, biking, hiking, praying, writing, talking, etc. You have to decide when are you going to sleep, what are you going to eat, what are you going to read, where are you going to bike, which path will you take during your hike, how will you pray, who will you write to, what will you say. Everything you do is preceded by a choice. If everything we do is preceded by a choice than HOW do we make choices? I pose this question because, if you do not know how to make choices, life could very quickly become challenging.

Choices are the results of our thoughts. Therefore, we make choices by thinking. Pretty profound, huh? Thinking can take place in a split second, for example when deciding to remove your hand from a hot stove before getting burned. Or it can take months, as in whether to change jobs or not. The outcome of our choices takes us to WHERE, that is to say, WHERE we are in life. Where do choices lead us? To exactly what we are experiencing right now – LIFE!

Which now means we can circle back to WHY do we make choices? We make choices to experience life. Now the wonderful truth that I have come to know through the life I have lived so far is that we can make our choices consciously or unconsciously. We can be aware of what is going on around us or we can be unaware. When we live consciously, we will find ourselves making significant choices with focused goals, like writing a book. That conscious choice is followed by hundreds of smaller choices that come together to manifest the original significant choice of writing a book. It is when we stay focused and conscious of the choices we are making that we can truly experience a purposeful life.

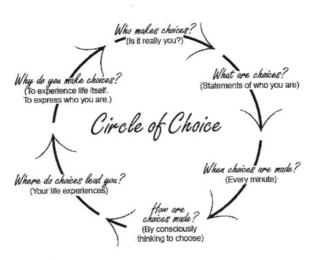

Illustrator: Bill Rehahn

We can actually experience life through our choices or we can just go through life. John Lennon exemplifies this wonderfully in his quote:

"Life is what happens to you while you're busy making other plans."

Said another way, we can be the cause of our own choices or we can live with the effect of everyone else's choices. This is why small, easy, spontaneous choices will generally not offer a fulfilling life. When all of your decisions are small, spontaneous, and easy, you probably are not living the highest life you could live. You may need to revisit the beginning of this chapter to consider WHO is making the choices. If your choices are all simple, you may be letting others make your choices for you. This can be a slippery slope when it comes to experiencing and living your highest self. If you believe you are living a fulfilled life letting everyone else make your choices for you, then go on living that way because it may be working for you. However, if you find yourself always blaming others for what is going on in your life, or you are faced with a difficult decision and cannot decide without getting an exorbitant amount of input from other people, or you always revert back to what Mom and Dad would do, or you are filled with envy when you see another person living the life you think you deserve, then you may want to read on.

Chapter 2:

Beingness Versus Doingness

Do you ever feel like your life is spiraling out of control and there is nothing you can do about it? Do you ever feel like you are on a slippery slope and you want to know how to stop yourself from going downhill faster? Have you ever been in a situation where you ask yourself why am I feeling or acting this way? Do you ever wonder where you are coming from? If we take the time to really think about it we can all recall times in our life when we have felt this way. We may not have felt it at exactly the time it was happening, but when we look back at it we can see it.

Once we see the problem, we may not know how to fix it, but we know we have felt it. That feeling is your soul trying to communicate with you. It is the deepest part of you saying,

> "Hey, I'm here and I can help you if you choose to listen to me."

When we feel a situation, or sometimes our whole life, spinning out of control, we can choose to come from that deeper part of ourselves or we can choose to let the situation drive itself and see where it leads us. In other words, we can be the Cause of what happens in our life or we can live with the Effects of our circumstances. When you turn to that deeper part of yourself and decide how you choose to act in a particular situation, you will find yourself living at the Cause of your life instead of at the Effects of it.

BEING is how you choose to act. Where you are "coming from" in any given situation is your state of beingness. DOING is the act itself. Your action in any given situation is doingness.

Your state of beingness determines what you will DO in a situation. More often than not, people have it backwards. They think that what they DO will bring them a particular feeling. But what they are feeling will bring about what they will DO.

Do you laugh to make yourself happy? Or cry to make yourself sad? No, the feeling precedes the action. You are happy, therefore, you laugh. You are sad, therefore, you cry. Or in my case, sometimes you are so happy you laugh so hard you cry!

How many times have you said to yourself

- "If only so-and-so would DO this or that, I could forgive them," or

- "If only my boss would acknowledge all the hard work I do, I would feel appreciated," or

- "If I could only DO this or DO that, I would BE happy."

- Etc., Etc.

The list could go on and on. But what would happen if you decided to BE forgiving, or appreciative, or happy without so-and-so doing anything, or without your boss' acknowledgement, or without doing this or that?

In my experience, if you choose your state of being first, then you will attract that feeling into your life. A positive state of being will attract positive experiences. If you are forgiving, you will draw that into your experience. If you are appreciative or happy, that will be drawn into your experience.

If you desire the experience of happiness, try BEING happy. If you would like someone to understand you, try being understanding. If you aim for joy in your life, do not DO joy. Instead, BE joyous and your actions will soon follow suit. In other words, you will begin to act in a joyous way toward yourself and others. From your state of beingness – joy – you will begin to do things that are joyful. You will find yourself smiling at people more often, greeting complete strangers with a cheerful "hello," sending a supportive note or email to a friend who is going through a tough time, seeing the beauty in the simple things in life – a baby's coo, a rose beginning to bloom, the sunset, a bird flying overhead, or the sound of excitement in your child's voice when they tell you about a new movie they saw.

This joyous energy will be expressed from you and cause others to be joyous around you, thus bringing joy back to yourself. It's a circle. What you ARE, you give away. What you give away, you experience. What you experience, you receive back.

All of life will take on new meaning when you come from your soul – that deeper part of you that says:

> "Hey I'm here; USE me. Choose to BE any part of Me (your SELF) and I (your SOUL) will help you to experience exactly that in your life."

Trying to create the experience first by doing something that will result in a feeling is a much more difficult process. To understand this, you must understand the three steps of creation.

Chapter 3:

Creation

"I think, therefore I am." ~~ *René Descartes*

This short quote speaks volumes. Put another way, by Neale Donald Walsch in <u>Conversations with God</u>, "You are what you think you are."

The first step of creation is thought. Everything in your life right now was once a thought. It could have been a conscious thought or a subconscious one. It could be your thought or the thought of another person in your life – a person you have drawn into your life to aid you in experiencing who you are.

That thought spoken, put into words, is the next step of creation. Once a thought is audible, either to you or another, it contains added energies. These energies are like the nutrients in the earth that help a seed to grow. The seed that is growing is your thought. The earth is the universe. Your thought has been pushed out into the universe with your words. You have planted the seed (thought) into the earth (universe) with your words.

Finally, that thought and those words will lead to action, the final step of creation. The action is you picking up your watering can and providing additional life blood to the seed and the nutrients of the earth with water. The seed, or thought, cannot survive on nutrients or words alone. It needs to be watered occasionally.

For that thought to truly become your experience it must be spoken about and acted on. It must be planted and watered. Therefore:

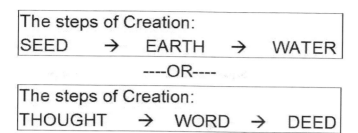

The steps of Creation:

SEED → EARTH → WATER

----OR----

The steps of Creation:

THOUGHT → WORD → DEED

Notice that the process was not water first, plant second, and THEN go get the seed. You have to start with the seed first. Have the thought first. From there will come your words and your actions.

Well, why does it work this way, you might ask? The seed contains everything within itself to become more of itself, to experience what it truly is. To create itself, the seed needs the nutrients of the earth and the water. The word and the deed are what must be present for the seed to become more of itself.

Without the thought (the seed), there is nothing to nurture. There is nothing to develop, nothing to grow, nothing to create. You would only have the nutrients of the earth (the word), and the water (the deed). Together, those only make MUD – More Unnecessary Doing. However, when they are utilized in combination with the seed, you create a BUD – a Being Using Divinity.

Would you prefer to have MUD in your life or a BUD? Whether you see a BUD as the beginning of a beautiful flower or as a close friend, either one is likely more desirable than a bunch of dirt!!

But how do I get a BUD in my life, you ask? Hold on. We're almost there, just one more chapter and then we will discuss the process of growing a BUD in your life.

Chapter 4:

Who Am I?

If you go back to the first chapter of this book, you will remember that choices start with thought. Thought is the first step in creation. Therefore, the choices you make create your experience. That can be a pretty tough pill to swallow if you have always looked at yourself as the victim, if you have always felt that everything others were thinking, saying, and doing has made your life the way that it is.

Remember: thought can be subconscious, and to let another make your choices for you is a choice itself. If you are ready to be truly honest with yourself about yourself, you can see where this kind of thinking can get you. I am willing to bet it is not WHERE you want to BE or WHO you want to BE!

After having read the first few chapters of this book, you might want to spend some time reflecting on who you currently are and what you are currently experiencing in life before you can move on with the process of choosing who you want to be.

Now that you have an understanding of choices, how they impact your life, the concept of beingness, and the process of creation, you might want to take some time to contemplate how choices, beingness, and creation have contributed to where you are in life.

Most likely, you will put the book down for some amount of time − an hour, a day, a week − ponder what you have just read and learned, and allow it to integrate into your thinking. You have always known all of this. You just needed a reminder, a repackaging of your own knowledge. Therefore, grant yourself the gift of time, and spend some quiet time alone each day reflecting on how these concepts have brought you to who you are and what you are experiencing today. Begin to realize how you arrived at where you are. See how your choices have shaped your life and how you have experienced life either through doingness or beingness. Rereading the Prologue can help. The story provides a real life example of how my choices and beingness created a life that was not what I wanted to experience.

By reflecting on the past, you can begin to see how true these concepts are. By understanding their truth, you can begin to take responsibility for the creation of what you are experiencing. This is a most difficult step because so many of us have lived our life on a subconscious level. Our thoughts, words, and actions have not come from a level of consciousness that we are willing to admit is there. Playing the victim or the martyr is safe and comfortable to us. Stepping up and taking responsibility causes us to leave our comfort zone. But it is when you leave your comfort zone that you truly begin to live.

Taking responsibility includes releasing your past. Not dwelling on it because you know you are NOT your past. You now realize you only drew the past to you to help you create who you are.

If you are comfortable and content with who you are, then continue living as you have been. However, if you find yourself discontent or not completely fulfilled, realize that this book ended up in your hands to help you. On either a subconscious or conscious level, you drew this book to you. You have given yourself the opportunity to choose who you want to be.

You can now take these concepts, proven true to you by your own life, and apply them to creating a different life. The only difference between your past and your future is the level of consciousness with which you choose to live.

Chapter 5:

The Process

Remember that the choices you make create your experience. That is what brought you to where you are today. It is also exactly what can bring you out of where you are and on the path to experiencing that higher self that you intuitively know is hiding inside of you. YOU think, YOU choose, YOU create, YOU experience. That is the process in a nutshell.

I did not make any promises that this was going to be some deeply philosophical or highly scientific process. It is a very simple one. Simple to talk about and simple to explain. A bit more difficult to apply to life. But I promise you that, once you honestly believe in this process and start applying it in your life, you will never go back.

You may be asking how do I think, choose, create, and experience? And how is that going to get me to experience a higher version of myself? Just exactly HOW do I apply this process? How long does it take? And when will I start seeing results? With those questions it sounds like we are going on a diet instead of a journey of self-creation. But I know those are questions you have because they are the same ones I had. So let's see if we can go through the process together.

Let's go back to the quotes at the beginning of the Creation chapter: *"I think, therefore I am"* and *"You are what you think you are."* What do these say to you? Sit for a few moments in complete quiet and just reflect. Repeat them to yourself.

For me, both of these statements speak about Beingness. I am joyful, therefore I express joy. I am kind, therefore I express kindness. I think I am angry, so I experience anger. I think I am frustrated, so I experience frustration. These states of being that we think about can be positive or negative.

Remember what we said before about states of being. They produce a circle. This energy, the state of being you choose, will be expressed from you and cause others to be that energy around you, thus bringing that energy back to yourself. It is a circle. What you ARE, you give away. What you give away, you experience. What you experience, you receive back.

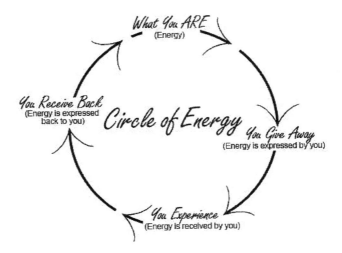

What You ARE
(Energy)

You Receive Back
(Energy is expressed
back to you)

Circle of Energy

You Give Away
(Energy is expressed by you)

You Experience
(Energy is received by you)

Illustrator: Bill Rehahn

You Think, You Choose

The first step in the process is to think about several different states of being and select which one (or two) you want to be. Who is it that you are creating? Which one would you like to experience in your life? Do you see yourself as honest, hopeful, helpful, humorous? Gracious, giving, grateful? The Aspects of Being chapter will help you to think of and reflect on many, many aspects of being. Thinking about states of being can be both fun and mind-boggling at the same time.

The following suggestions might help you narrow down or focus on the specific one or two you want to experiment with:

Take one a day (not a vitamin!).

- Read what is presented in The Aspects of Being chapter, if it is an aspect that I defined.

- Sit quietly for a few minutes and think about that one aspect.

- Say it aloud to yourself several times. Allow your body to feel the vibrational sound of the word.

- Write out, in a few sentences, your own description or definition of what that aspect means for you.
  - o Is this what you choose to display to the world?
  - o Is this what you choose to experience in your life?
  - o Is this how you see yourself?

- Think about people in your life that you think exhibit that aspect. Write a little bit about that person.
  - o Who are they?
  - o Is this someone you admire?
  - o What have they done in their life that causes you to link them with this aspect?
  - o Are they experiencing something in their life that you would like to experience?

- While you are getting dressed, packing lunches, driving, waiting in line, going through the mail, cooking dinner, putting the kids to bed, think about that aspect of being.

- Enlist the help of your kids, grab some old magazines, some markers, and some glue and make a collage of words and pictures that exemplify that aspect. Or if you do not have kids do it yourself. Adults can get sticky with the glue too.

- Jump on the internet and search that aspect, see what you find.

- Ask different people throughout the day what that word means to them. LISTEN to what they say.

- Find a song with that word in the title and listen to it.

- Go to the library and search out a children's book with that word in the title. Read it. Children's stories are not only written to entertain children.

- Search out a movie with that aspect in the title. Watch the movie. Movies are definitely not made to only entertain; more often than not, they contain powerful messages.

These are only suggestions. Some people may be able to review the aspects and very quickly choose which one they intend to manifest in their life. If that is not you, it is completely OK. Give yourself time and have some fun with this. After all, this is the biggest CHOICE in the entire process. This is the thought, the seed, that starts it all. From this, you will become the BUD – you will be a Being Using Divinity.

Once you have thought about and reflected on several states of being, choose which one you would like to experience. One that you believe best exhibits who you choose to be.

You Create

It is time to reflect on what that aspect of being that you chose would look like to you. You may find it helpful to write out your answers to these questions.

- Who would you be if you came from that state of being in every aspect of your life? For example, if you chose honesty, ask yourself how an honest person would live their life?

- What kind of *thoughts* would you have?

- What kind of *words* would you speak?

- What kind of *actions* would you take?

Did you catch what three nouns I used? Can you see where this is going?

Now comes the hard part. Once you have chosen the state of being you think best exhibits who you want to be, you must create it. Now you may say but how do I create patience? How do I create gratitude? How do I create joy? The key to this step is NOT to DO but to BE. It is in the being that you will create. Go back to the Circle of Energy drawing at the beginning of this chapter and study it. It really does work this way. Be patient, be grateful, be joyous and you will create those feelings for others and thus for yourself. If you are like me, you are still asking, HOW??? How do I "give away" patience? How do I share the energy of patience with others?

Here is how. The moment you make the choice to create a particular form of energy in your life, the universe will begin to help you out. The universe will provide for you a contextual field in which to create. In our relative world, we define things by their opposites, referred to as the Law of Polarity. To understand cold, you must understand hot. To understand tall, you must understand short. Each item is defined by its relationship to its opposite.

Therefore, the universe will provide you the exact opposite energy form to enable you the chance to choose the opposite of what you are experiencing. You will have the opportunity to express your chosen energy to another. You will be allowed to express your chosen state of being because the exact opposite of it will continue to appear in your life.

This is exemplified in the following:

I asked for strength
and God gave me difficulties to make me strong.

I asked for wisdom
and God gave me problems to solve.

I asked for prosperity
and God gave me brawn and brain to work.

I asked for courage
and God gave me dangers to overcome.

I asked for patience
and God placed me in situations
where I was forced to wait.

I asked for love
and God gave me troubled people to help.

I asked for favors
and God gave me opportunities.

I asked for everything so I could enjoy life.
Instead, He gave me life
so I could enjoy everything.

I received nothing I wanted
I received everything I needed.

My prayer has been answered.

~~Author Unknown

This act of being (creation) does take some monitoring. It may take thinking and re-thinking, choosing and re-choosing that state of being. When thinking, speaking, and acting, you will need to stop and say to yourself how would a _____ person think, speak or act in this situation. You fill in the blank with the aspect of being you chose. However, it is through this constant monitoring you become CONSCIOUS, that is, SELF-conscious. You consciously begin to CREATE who you are, your-SELF. Gone will be the days of being influenced by the thinking and choices of others. Now it is your turn. You ask the question, who am I? And what would I think, say, or do? You think, you choose, you create.

You Experience

Over time, the monitoring will not necessarily be minute to minute, hour to hour, as it is in the beginning. That is because this consciousness, this level of creation, will become a part of your experience, the last step of the process.

You will begin to experience who you truly are and who you truly choose to be. The most wonderful part of this process is that, once you experience this with one aspect, you come to a remembering. When you remember that you can choose who you are, you open the door to unlimited possibilities.

It is at this point that you may realize that you have been hiding from yourself and the rest of the world. You will begin to see yourself as that iceberg – so much of yourself hidden under the surface of the water. You come to understand that the biggest limitation to becoming who you choose to be is YOU. At the same time, or in my case over the course of time, you will recognize that the process you used to create yourself is the same one you can use to begin to move that iceberg up out of the water. You can continue to create and demonstrate more and more of yourself to the world simply by choosing to.

Recall in Chapter 3: Creation, that when you combined thought, word, and action, or the seed, the nutrients, and the water, you would have a BUD, a Being Using Divinity. That little seed, nurtured by the earth and water, would poke through for all the world to see as a beautiful flower. Instead of continuing to be that iceberg and hiding so much of yourself, you can choose to be that Being Using Divinity and let your true self surface and rise for all the world to see and experience.

Once you have mastered one or two aspects of being, you can use your exhilaration to expand into other areas. You will not be content to just "poke through." You will continue to grow that BUD into even more magnificence. You will realize that there is nothing stopping you from experiencing all positive aspects of life. All those aspects that you used to believe could not possibly be yours to experience. This realization will be made with immense gratitude to God, for it is He who has created this experience called life and given us the opportunity to choose the paths we travel.

You will realize that the decision is all up to you. No one is going to come into your life and tell you what you are supposed to DO to experience a greater version of yourself, to evolve and create that person you were meant to BE. Only you can choose, consciously choose, every day, every hour, every minute to BE who you are.

Chapter 6:

The Question

Do I choose MUD or BUD? This is the golden question that can trigger the process.

You Think
You Choose
You Create
You Experience

As you move through your day, pause momentarily and ask yourself the question. Do I choose More Unnecessary Doing (MUD) or Being Using Divinity (BUD)? THINK about it! Do you choose to operate on auto-pilot reaction? Or divine creation?

Auto-pilot reaction inevitably leads to More Unnecessary Doing, while divine creation comes from a Being Using Divinity. However you define divinity is up to you. For me, it is the essence of a power or energy greater than I am that resides within me. When I invoke that essence through choice, I co-create with God and begin to experience Heaven on Earth.

Now, that may sound too religious for some. So here is a different perspective. Have you ever experienced blissful happiness with a close friend, someone you love (a "bud") based on something you created together? Perhaps it was making delicious cookies with your child, winning a championship game, having sex. OK, I knew that would get your attention! That "blissful happiness" is Heaven on Earth and the person you shared the experience with is God, in human form.

If you took a moment to think before acting/doing, which would you choose? MUD or BUD? Is the life you desire filled with More Unnecessary Doing or will you be a Being Using Divinity? Will you operate from auto-pilot reaction or divine creation?

In fact, look at the words REACTION and CREATION. When you move from MUD to BUD, or auto-pilot reaction to divine creation, you simply move the "C" to the front. That "C" stands for conscious or choice or most appropriate to this process, conscious choice.

<u>Think</u> about it!!

Make the choice of MUD or BUD *first* and then watch what you create and experience in your life!!

Chapter 7:

Aspects of Being

This chapter contains thoughts and visuals of various aspects of being. For each aspect, the section will include:

- the state of beingness

- my thoughts about the meaning or descriptions of how I have experienced that aspect of being in my life

- ideas about the aspect of beingness in the form of quotes

- a picture of what that aspect might look like or an image that might produce that feeling within you when you look at it

Because the list of beingness can be endless and you want to start working with the process instead of just reading about it, the last section of this chapter contains a list of additional aspects of being without any commentary. You are free to add your own commentary, search out your own quotes, and find your own pictures. Feel free to add to the list.

While reading through the list, say each one aloud. Take a moment with each word. Which ones bring up stronger feelings than others? If you are truly honest with yourself, you will probably see that there is a part of you that identifies with every word on this list, because in effect we are all of it.

At some point in your life, you have been, are now, or will be each one of these aspects. At our highest level, we desire to EXPERIENCE each of these aspects, not just to know them but to experience them.

You will quickly notice that this chapter only discusses positive aspects of being. Fortunately for us, we currently live in a relative world. That means that for every positive aspect of being, a negative aspect of being also exists. One cannot, in the world of the relative, exist without the other.

"You cannot experience that which you are, in the absence of that which you are not," as <u>Conversations with God</u> so succinctly puts it.

I chose to focus on positive aspects of being because I believe that if a person is making a conscious choice about who they want to be, it is within their human nature to select a positive characteristic. But I do want to caution you, as is explained in the "You Create" step of the process, once you select one of these states of consciousness, be prepared for the exact opposite to show up in your life. That is because, as I stated before, we live in a relative world. You cannot experience happiness without being shown sadness. You may not have to experience every negative aspect in order to experience the opposite, but you will have to witness it in some way.

Compassion

Compassion is understanding what another is feeling, seeing yourself in their situation, realizing you cannot make the pain go away but that they are still loved by you. Being present for the other either physically or in thought, via a hug or a prayer. You can have compassion for someone you know or a complete stranger whose story you see on TV or read about in a magazine. A compassionate person knows that the tears will again one day dry and that the tears can be a stepping stone for growth and evolution. A compassionate person gives hope because they understand that growth can come through crisis.

Until he extends his circle of compassion to all living things, man will not find peace.
~~Albert Schweitzer

Compassion arises from imagination, which can leap over the boundaries of differences between us and find the common ground we share.
~~David Spangler, Parent as Mystic, Mystic as Parent

Compassion

Hope

Hope is the strength you see in another person and the gentle nudge you give the person so that they too can see the strength within themselves. Sometimes the strength you see is in yourself and you nudge yourself into knowing that you can be who you choose to be. Once you see the strength in yourself or in another, kindness tends to take over.

Hope is the thing with feathers --/ That perches in the soul --/ And sings the tunes without the words --/ And never stops --at all --.
~~Emily Dickinson, US poet, The Complete Poems of Emily Dickinson

Things start out as hopes and end up as habits.
~~Lillian Hellman

Hope

Source O. George "Frenchy" DuPuis

Kindness

Kindness is showing that you care. It is living the golden rule of, "Do unto others what you would have them do unto you." It can be as simple as a smile to someone or as big as taking in a homeless person for the night. It is that act that says to someone, "You matter."

Kind words can be short and easy to speak, but their echoes are truly endless.
~~Mother Teresa

No act of kindness, no matter how small, is ever wasted.
~~Aesop

Kindness is more than deeds. It is an attitude, an expression, a look, a touch. It is anything that lifts another person.
~~C. Neil Strait

Kindness is an inner desire that makes us want to do good things even if we do not get anything in return. It is the joy of our life to do them. When we do good things from this inner desire, there is kindness in everything we think, say, want and do.
~~Emanuel Swedenborg

Kindness

Source O. George "Frenchy" DuPuis

Gentleness

Gentleness is the expression of the strength of your soul, not the strength of your physical body. To be gentle towards another is to be willing to tap into that maternal instinct, that feminine side of yourself, and to be a bit vulnerable. Share touch with another person when only human touch can accomplish what words cannot. Use the softness of your voice to calm another's anger. Realize the importance of giving your full attention to someone who thinks no one ever listens. To experience gentleness, open yourself to the gentleness of God. The touch of a child's hand on your face, the hum of a mother as she rocks her newborn baby to sleep in her arms, the breeze against your body as you stand on the shoreline, the warmth of the sun on your face as it sets: these are times when the gentleness of God is experienced.

Only the weak are cruel. Gentleness can only be expected from the strong.
~~Leo F. Buscaglia

There is nothing stronger in the world than gentleness.
~~Han Suyin, A Many Splendored Thing

Gentleness

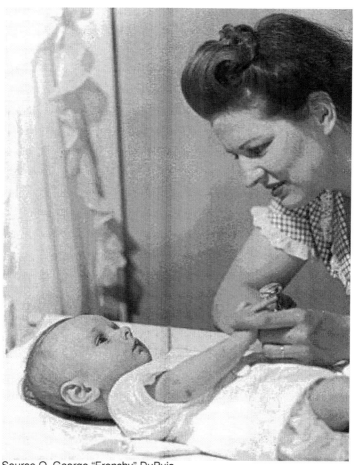

Source O. George "Frenchy" DuPuis

Forgiveness

Forgiveness is seeing the perfection in all things. Realizing that there are no victims, there are only miracles and angels in our lives. Even in the worst of circumstances, we are provided with an opportunity to show a part of ourselves, that we might remember who we are and what we are capable of.

Forgiveness is unlocking the door to set someone free and realizing you were the prisoner!
~~Max Lucado

Sincere forgiveness isn't colored with expectations that the other person apologize or change. Don't worry whether or not they finally understand you. Love them and release them. Life feeds back truth to people in its own way and time.
~~Sara Paddison

Forgiveness

Patience

Patience is tolerance. It means being able to accept differences in understanding. Realizing everyone will not see the world as you do, but also realizing that without judgment.

At first, I found it humorous that I chose this aspect of being because I certainly do not seem to have any...patience, that is. I do not have patience in the purest form, the ability to wait until someone "gets" something. I always said I could never teach because I did not have the patience. If someone did not understand something I was explaining, I would become impatient. But after some thought, I realized that as I have spiritually matured, patience has taken on new meaning for me. It is acceptance of differences. It is tolerance. And this I do have.

Patience with others is Love, Patience with self is Hope, Patience with God is Faith.
~~Adel Bestavros

Mine is not a better way, mine is merely another way.
~~Neale Donald Walsch, Conversations With God

Self-Truth and Authenticity

Self-truth is a gut-level calling. It is a knowing who you are and being willing to live that every day of your life, no matter what others think, say, or do. It is living your authentic self. Your self-truth is that part of yourself that shows up when you least expect it. It is the part of you that keeps knocking on the door but you are not answering. Instead you are ignoring it as something too wild, or "there's no way I could do that." Do not keep the door closed. Be willing to open it up and see what that part of yourself has to say to you. If you are willing to truly listen and believe, you will be surprised by what can happen in your life.

Say not, "I have found the truth," but rather, "I have found a truth."
~~Kahlil Gibran

Never apologize for showing feeling. When you do so, you apologize for the truth.
~~Benjamin Disraeli

The pursuit of truth will set you free; even if you never catch up with it.
~~Unknown

Know your truth and your truth shall set you free.
~~Unknown

Self-truth and Authenticity

Faith and Trust

Faith is knowing that there is a force greater than you in the Universe that knows where you are supposed to go and what you came here for. Trust in that force. Trust not only your experience but, more importantly, your feelings. Do not judge your feelings, trust them, it will lead you down your path more quickly than you would expect.

All I have seen teaches me to trust the Creator for all I have not seen.
~~Ralph Waldo Emerson

To one who has faith, no explanation is necessary.
To one without faith, no explanation is possible.
~~St. Thomas Aquinas

Faith is trust in what the spirit learned eons ago.
~~B.H. Roberts

I believe though I do not comprehend, and I hold by faith what I cannot grasp with the mind.
~~St. Bernard

Faithless is he who quits when the road darkens.
~~J.R.R. Tolkien, Lord of the Rings

Faith and Trust

Source O. George "Frenchy" DuPuis

Courage

Courage is the strength needed to live your truth. It is the ability to say, "This is who I am and this is who I choose to be." Courage goes hand-in-hand with the truth and trust discussed earlier. Once you know your truth, and trust your feelings, it takes a great deal of courage to stand up and say, "This is who I am and this is who I choose to be." But hold on to that courage because, if you do, your life will soon begin to be a testimony to your truth and others will not be able to argue with that. They will see who you are, and your life lived, and decide for themselves that they too can live as consciously as you are. You will not have to DO anything – you will just have to BE.

The real acid test of courage is to be just your honest self when everybody is trying to be like somebody else.
~~Andrew Jensen

We need to find the courage to say NO to the things and people that are not serving us if we want to rediscover ourselves and live our lives with authenticity.
~~Barbara De Angelis

Is he alone who has courage on his right hand and faith on his left hand?
~~Charles A. Lindbergh

Courage is not the absence of fear, but rather the judgment that something else is more important than fear.
~~Ambrose Redmoon

All your dreams come true, if you have the courage to pursue them.
~~Walt Disney

Helpfulness

Helpfulness is a willingness to listen, to understand, and to validate another human being. This is one of my favorites. When I started out in this process of conscious choices, I chose helpfulness and joy as my states of being. I choose to be nothing more than helpful. I had learned so much on my spiritual journey that I could not keep it inside anymore. I had to put it out there. I had to help others realize what they too were capable of. Once I opened up to this, those who needed help spiritually showed up in my life. I wore my heart (my spirituality) on my sleeve and others saw that. They were able to come to me, sometimes in a vulnerable state, and knew I would provide whatever help I could. I was not handing them a set of instructions on how to fix themselves. My helpfulness was a willingness to listen, to understand, to validate them. I let them know that they were not the only ones out there feeling that way, and that there was nothing wrong with being confused or lost. Sometimes it is the best place to be. It is in that place that you are sometimes the most willing to listen AND hear. Most importantly, I tried to assist them by allowing them to realize the *fix* would come from within themselves if they were willing to be open to it and listen to the answers that God may be providing to them.

Treat people as if they were what they should be, and you help them become what they are capable of becoming.
~~Johann Goethe

Treat people like angels; you will meet some and help make some.
~~Max Lucado

Joy

"I define joy as a sustained sense of well-being and internal peace — a connection to what matters. Real joy, like real power, as Gary Zukav describes it, happens 'when your personality comes to fully serve the energy of your soul'."
~~Oprah Winfrey, May 2001 O Magazine.

A better definition of joy I could not find, much less write myself. So, I will say, "Thanks, Oprah," because you have helped me create who I am today.

I read that passage on my way to a retreat and it resonated profoundly with me. It was on that retreat that I was first asked to choose a state of being and BE that for a half hour and see what changed in my life. Since I had resonated with that passage, I chose Joy. During the exercise something inside me clicked, my truth I believe, and I did not stop being joyful after a half hour — in fact, I never stopped. It was that simple exercise that led to this book.

It is my purpose in life to bring joy; that sense of internal peace, to every individual I meet. It is my belief that world peace starts at the individual level. It starts with inner peace. As we achieve inner peace and resonate that throughout our community by who we are, then we begin the ripple effect of accomplishing world peace.

The joy in life is to be used for a purpose. I want to be used up when I die.
~~George Bernard Shaw

There is no greater joy nor greater reward than to make a fundamental difference in someone's life.
~~Sister Mary Rose McGeady

Real joy comes not from ease or riches or from the praise of men, but from doing something worthwhile.
~~Pierre Coneille

Joy

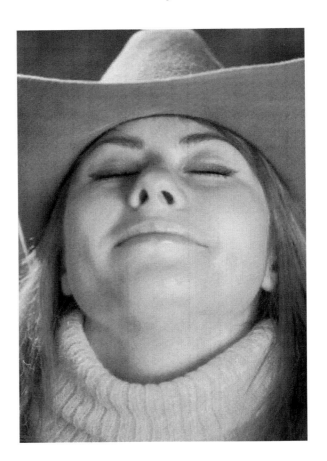

*Wisdom
and
Clarity*

Wisdom is taking what you have learned in your experiences and applying it to your daily life and the lives of all those with whom you come in contact. But clarity comes in when you offer your wisdom in such a way that does not say,

> "Do it this way, or else."

But rather it says,

> "Try this, and see if this works for you. If it does not that's OK. Keep questioning and you will be led to the answer when you are ready."

Knowledge is that which is acquired by learning.
Wisdom is knowing what to do with it.
~~Author Unknown

Wisdom is knowledge which has become a part of one's being.
~~Orison Swett Marden

Wisdom is the power to put our time and our knowledge to the proper use.
~~Thomas J. Watson

Wisdom and Clarity

Understanding

Understanding involves hearing, not just listening but hearing. It is being willing to hear what the other person is saying and allowing yourself to interpret the situation from their perspective, not your own. Judgment does not need to follow; you can simply observe.

Understanding does not always involve another person. Often, you must be understanding with yourself. Allow yourself the chance to feel a certain way. Do not judge it; just feel it, observe it. Be understanding with yourself. Afterwards, see if it worked for you. What does this feeling say about you? Is this who you used to be? Is this who you are now? Is it who you choose to be in the future?

Yearn to understand first and to be understood second.
~~Beca Lewis Allen

When we talk about understanding, surely it takes place only when the mind listens completely – the mind being your heart, your nerves, your ears – when you give your whole attention to it.
~~Jiddu Krishnamurti

Understanding

Sharing
and
Connecting

Sharing is giving of yourself. Connecting is the link between the giver and the receiver. By allowing ourselves to share with others, we allow ourselves to connect with others.

This sharing can take place in many ways, sharing material things, sharing our thoughts, our ideas, our experiences. By sharing, we say to the other person, "This is who I am," we connect with them. When we are open to sharing of ourselves, or our possessions, or our talents, etc. we often find that this opens the door for the other person to share with us. This strengthens the connection we feel with them.

This sharing and connecting can happen on many levels from running into each other at the coffee station and exchanging words about the past weekend, to donating to your favorite charity, to sharing your excitement about an upcoming event in your life, to sharing your deepest desires with your best friend, to sharing your deepest fears with yourself and God. When we have a willingness to be vulnerable and open to sharing, we allow ourselves the chance to connect with others and that connection can speed up the evolutionary process for all those involved.

The greatest good you can do for another is not just to share your riches, but to reveal to him his own.
~~Benjamin Disraeli

Live your life from your heart. Share from your heart. And your story will touch and heal people's souls.
~~Melody Beattie

Sharing and Connecting

Peace

Peace is knowing you are part of a master, Divine plan. But it is a flexible master plan. Peace is knowing that no matter what path you choose, have chosen, or will choose, you will always be led to exactly where you are supposed to be.

Be at peace with yourself first and then you will be able to bring peace to others.
~~Thomas A. Kempis

Peace is not the absence of trouble, but the presence of God.
~~Steve Dow

When you find peace within yourself, you become the kind of person who can live at peace with others.
~~Peace Pilgrim

Peace is the deliberate adjustment of my life to the will of God.
~~Source Unknown

Peace

Caring

Caring is that aspect that allows you to validate another; to let them know that you understand how they could feel the way they feel, say whatever it is that they say, act the way they act. You understand from their current perspective why they feel, say, and act, in the way that they do. But through your caring, you are able to allow them to re-validate what is going on and see if it is working for them.

Dr. Phil McGraw is great at this when he asks,

"Well, how's that working for you?"

It sums up the idea of,

"I understand how you could feel that way, but is there another way to feel?"

You do not even have to tell them another way to feel – let them come up with it, allowing the person to see that there may be another perspective, not a right or wrong perspective, just another perspective. Once they are able to see another way, they can make a choice as to which way works better for who they are and who they want to be.

As with all the other aspects of being, this is not something you can only *be* with another person. You can *be* caring with yourself. Validate your own feelings but notice if they are serving you. Sometimes you just have to let the feeling be, notice that it is there, realize it's OK, and allow yourself the time to move to another way. When you do this, *you are truly taking <u>care</u> of your-self.*

Perhaps we're too embarrassed to change or too frightened of the consequences of showing that we actually care. But why not risk it anyway? Begin today. Carry out a random act of seemingly senseless kindness, with no expectation or reward or punishment. Safe in the knowledge that one day, someone somewhere might do the same for you.
~~Princess Diana

Too often we underestimate the power of a touch, a smile, a kind word, a listening ear, an honest compliment, or the smallest act of caring, all of which have the potential to turn a life around.
~~Leo F. Buscaglia

Love

Love is the all of everything. I have purposely left the best for last. Read everything before this and you will have my definition of love. It is a combination of every aspect of being we have ever felt, expressed and experienced. It is the sum total of who we are, why we are here, and the only thing we take with us when we leave. With love, we can BE everything; without love, we are nothing. Yet everything includes nothing, right? Therefore, we are never NOT love; it is just a matter of how we choose to express it.

We come into the world having nothing, but everything we need is within us. Have you ever looked into the eyes of a newborn child? There is only love there. As we move through the experiences of life we can choose to remember what we already knew before we entered life, love is all there is, and it does not come from outside ourselves, from "things" – it comes from within.

We can choose to spend our lives attaining every *thing* we think we need, forgetting it is already inside us, and end up leaving the world with nothing. Or we can remember that love resides within us and does not come from having *things* at all. It comes from who we are and how we express who we are to the world. How we choose to express, or bring love *out of ourselves*, is all up to us.

When you choose to remember that love resides within you, and you express that love throughout your life, you leave the world with everything. I mean that two ways – you leave everything you are to those whose lives you touched and you take everything that you are with you.

Love is what's in the room with you at Christmas if you stop opening presents and listen.
~~Bobby - age 5

Love is the one word that we use every day, and the one word that words cannot define.
~~Anna K. Schwartz

To love for the sake of being loved is human; to love for the sake of loving is angelic.
~~Alphonse de Lamartine

You can give without loving, but you cannot love without giving.
~~Amy Carmichael

Love is something eternal; the aspect may change, but not the essence.
~~Vincent Van Gogh

Love

Now it is your turn. Here are several other aspects of being you may choose to examine.

You can be:

Accepting	Humorous
Adventurous	Insightful
Beautiful	Inspiring
Blessed	Intimate
Comforting	Magnificent
Concerned	Marvelous
Confident	Open
Creative	Optimistic
Free	Passionate
Generous	Respectful
Grateful	Responsible
Happy	Simple
Harmonious	Sincere
Healed	Strong
Honest	Tender
Honorable	Whole
Humble	Willing

Chapter 8:

Who Do I Choose to Be?

You may recall at the beginning of the book I said I was a sucker for a good story. It is why I love to read and watch movies. So, to illustrate a few of these concepts, let me tell you a story.

In the movie, "City of Joy," Patrick Swayze skillfully and soulfully portrays the character of Max Lowe, an American doctor who travels to India to find answers. Who is he? Why is he here? Through his relationships with two unlikely characters, he is given the opportunity to decide who he is and create his reason for BEING here.

Max first meets Joan at her clinic when he awakens after he has been beaten up and robbed. Joan is a nurse who consciously chooses to express her boundless love with an entire community by running a free health clinic in the slums of Calcutta.

Learning that Max is a doctor, Joan convinces him to stay temporarily and help her with the clinic. As their friendship develops, Joan's actions and words teach Max a great deal about who is making the choices in his life. She sees that Max has lived his life always doing what others expected of him. When Max implies that she must be crazy for purposely living and working in such conditions she tells him,

"I'm here because I want to be here."

On the steps of the clinic Joan explains her life philosophy to Max.

"I believe in life we really only have three choices: to run, to spectate, or to commit."

Later, Max decides to be a "running spectator" and Joan reminds him that "you can't leave your demons behind, they'll chase after you." In other words, you have to be willing to confront and release your past.

As Joan sees how past choices and experiences have influenced how Max defines himself, Max begins to see how past conditioning has adversely impacted his new friend, Hasari Pal. During his time working at the clinic, Max grows to love Hasari's family.

Hasari is a rickshaw puller who lives in the village where Joan runs her clinic. It is Hasari who first brings Max to the clinic after witnessing Max's run-in with a local gang.

Hasari struggles with the safety of playing the victim. He believes he is a small man with a small fate and cannot see himself taking a stand against corrupt authority.

Through Max's encouragement and generosity, Hasari is able to let go of this belief and choose to BE someone else, someone of strength. As the safety of his family is threatened right before his eyes, Hasari finds the strength within himself to be the cause of change and stand up to the local authorities, not only for his family but for his entire village.

Seeing the entire community celebrate their victory over the local authorities and the freedom that brings them, Max understands what Joan has been telling him and what he has witnessed through Hasari's courage. **When each person chooses who they will be, and commits to that choice, they have the power to create the life they desire.**

During the celebration, Joan says to Max,

> "You are free to go."
> He replies, "No, I'm free to stay."

He has chosen not to run, not to spectate, but to commit.

Throughout the film, we learn that Hasari's greatest desire is to give his children a better life and Max wants nothing more than to experience the love of family and help those in need through his medical skills. To live the lives they desire, both men must choose to let go of their past, see the impact it has had on who they are, and how it will continue to influence their life if they allow it to. When they choose to share who they are and give what they have, what they desire is manifested in their lives.

And so it is with you!

When Max first finds himself at the clinic he asks Joan,

> "Where am I at?"
> Joan replies, "The City of Joy."
> He asks, "Is that spiritual or geographical?"
> Her answer is, "It's all in your point of view."

His question is not one she can answer directly. It has to come from within him. It has to be experienced on a personal level.

Much the same as the question, "Who do I choose to be?" It is all in your perspective. **You must choose from within yourself who you will be. When you live that choice consciously you create and experience who you are.**

Chapter 9:

The Light in Your Soul

We can chart our future clearly and wisely only when we know the path which has led to the present.
~~Adlai E. Stevenson

The path that has led to your present is clearly the result of <u>choices</u> you have made in life. Now it is your turn to make different choices, conscious choices. It is time to chart your future, to realize the importance that thought plays in your experience. We as human beings do create our own reality. Is your reality an iceberg? Or is it a Being Using Divinity? The choice is yours.

When you are clear and consistent in your thoughts, your words and actions will follow. When you harness your thoughts, you see that you have the ability to create your own experience. That means consciously choosing and re-choosing who you are and who you choose to be. It means waking each morning and saying, "I choose to be _____ today." (You fill in the blank.) While you are going through your morning routine, think about how that aspect of being will reveal itself to you throughout the day. When things are going haywire, take a moment to stop, to think, to say, "I choose to be _____." Uttering those words aloud can have tremendous power for you. Remember, words are creative.

At the end of a tiring day you might hear yourself saying, "I wasn't very _____ today." Go and find a way to give that aspect of being to another because actions are creative, too. The fastest way to experience something in your life is to give it to another. Remember the Circle of Energy from Chapter 5 – when you share energy with someone, it comes back to you. It might not come back immediately, but it will come back, usually when you need it most.

The key to this whole process is to be OPEN. Open your mind to the wisdom inside yourself. Give your soul a chance to participate in your life. Give it the chance to say, "Hi." You will be amazed at what you are capable of being, and thus doing, in your life.

Open your mind to God's wisdom, open your soul to God's peace, open your heart to God's love and all three will stay with you forever.
~~Mary Stavros

My purpose in writing this book is to help you to understand how you can create the life you choose. In so doing, I hope to give you back a piece, or a peace, of yourself. Hopefully, as you begin to see one piece of yourself, you will choose to explore more pieces. Eventually you will choose the aspect of being called Peace and you will experiment with that in your life.

You see, I honestly believe that a peaceful world starts at the individual level. When you experience inner peace, you have a ripple effect on all those who meet you. I also believe that we, as a world, are at a turning point in our existence, and just like individuals can CHOOSE to create their experience, we as a world can COLLECTIVELY create the results that we CHOOSE at this pivotal time in our history. We CAN change the world, one person at a time.

I have actually been called "Pollyanna" for my thinking when I have discussed this change the world idea with others. The truth is my former self would have been discouraged by such statements. I would have thought,

> "Yeah, they're probably right, I am out of my mind, how can one measly little person change the world?"

But I have found that it is exactly when people say I am out of my mind that I find I am really listening to my soul and then I know it is what I have to do, it is who I am. It is when people called me Pollyanna that it made me more determined to finish this book and get my idea out there.

If I am able to help only one person realize they can have the life they choose, I will have accomplished what I set out to do. I will have begun to change the world, one person at a time.

If there is light in the soul,
There will be beauty in the person.

If there is beauty in the person,
There will be harmony in the house.

If there is harmony in the house,
There will be order in the nation.

If there is order in the nation,
There will be peace in the world.

~~Chinese Proverb

I hope I have helped you find the light in your soul.

###

My Choices Journal

These pages are provided to help and support you along your Conscious Choices journey.

You may choose to use the following pages to:
- reflect on the choices you have made throughout your life
- explore the conscious choices you intent to make going forward
- define additional Aspects of Being
- capture quotes that you have found

Or you may decide to use these pages as a bit of a diary to write out your thoughts about the aspect of being you chose to play with (for the day or the week) and then record the experiences you had with that aspect of being.

Whatever you choose, know that you are fully supported as you create who you choose to BE!!

My Choices Journal

My Choices Journal

_____

_____

_____

_____

_____

_____

_____

_____

_____

_____

My Choices Journal

_____

_____

_____

_____

_____

_____

_____

_____

_____

_____

My Choices Journal

My Choices Journal

_____

_____

_____

_____

_____

_____

_____

_____

_____

_____

My Choices Journal

My Choices Journal

About the Author

Celeste currently resides in Macomb, Michigan (USA) with her son, Christopher. She enjoys traveling, movies, reading, country music, being surrounded by nature, and watching her son's hockey games. A Reiki practitioner since 2003, she loves to use her gifts as tools for spiritual growth. Her dream is to share her unique energy work with those in the entertainment industry to raise the consciousness of the planet.

Please visit *http://www.myconsciouschoices.com* to learn more and further explore the concepts shared here.